Curiou
and the
Mystery Boxes

by Jefferson Greene
illustrated by Greg Paprocki

 HOUGHTON MIFFLIN   BOSTON

Printed in the U.S.A.

ISBN 10: 0-618-88645-1
ISBN 13: 978-0-618-88645-6

123456789 STA 16 15 14 13 12 11 10 09 08 07

George heard a knock.
Two boxes had arrived.

Which box looks heavier?

George was curious.
He picked up the small box.

Which box looks lighter? 3

George tried the big box.
It was too heavy.

Will George find more or less in the big box?

George opened the small box.
He found apples. Delicious!

Which box holds less?

He opened the big box.
Bananas! His favorite!

Which box holds more?

Uh-Oh! Empty Boxes!
"George! You silly monkey."

Drawing Boxes

Draw Categorize and Classify
   Draw a picture of what was in the small box on page 5.

Tell About
   Tell someone why George could not lift the big box shown on page 4.

Write
   Write which box had more fruit in it.